The Sunflower

PRINCIPLE

Life Lessons *from*
a Simple Flower

DONNA
AUSTIN

Inspiring Voices®
A Service of **Guideposts**

Inspiring Voices books may be ordered through booksellers or by contacting:

Inspiring Voices
1663 Liberty Drive
Bloomington, IN 47403
www.inspiringvoices.com
1-(866) 697-5313

Because of the dynamic nature of the Internet, any web addresses or links contained in this book may have changed since publication and may no longer be valid. The views expressed in this work are solely those of the author and do not necessarily reflect the views of the publisher, and the publisher hereby disclaims any responsibility for them.

Any people depicted in stock imagery provided by Thinkstock are models, and such images are being used for illustrative purposes only.

Certain stock imagery © Thinkstock.

ISBN: 978-1-4624-0278-6 (sc)
ISBN: 978-1-4624-0277-9 (e)

Library of Congress Control Number: 2012914914

Printed in the United States of America

Inspiring Voices rev. date: 9/20/2012

If you have received this book as a gift, it means that you have been observed sowing the four Sunflower Principle seeds into the life of another. That officially makes you a sunflower! Thank you for sharing your gifts of service.

The Sunflower Principle is my gift to you,
because you have been a sunflower to me.

(Insert signature & date line)

_____

Donna Austin's story about the "Sunflower Principle" inspires us to examine the gift of friendship. Donna's own "friendship bouquet" is gigantic and vibrant because she has been doing exactly what she asks of us. May her inspiration become ours, and may "Sunflower Groups" spring up everywhere!

June Williams, Educator

Donna Austin celebrates the gift of deep personal friendships, as she exposes her authentic life experiences and creates the opportunity for the reader to reflect on the relationships in his/her life. This inspirational view of relationships reveals opportunities to sow the seeds of compassion, love, peace, and understanding.

Jackie McBride, Ed. D.

Principle:

Merriam-Webster.com/dictionary defines the word principle as follows:

    a: a comprehensive and fundamental law, doctrine, or assumption

    b: (1): a rule or code of conduct (2) habitual devotion to right principles.

Introduction: *The Sunflower Principle*

After I recovered from the ashes of divorce that destroyed my family of twenty-five years, I fell in love again. My love affair was with a bunch of big, bold, and beautiful sunflowers. I learned many valuable lessons in my garden tending to these simple flowers. They taught me how to withstand the storms of life, how to lift my head, to stand tall again with the confidence to face another day. I learned the importance of building relationships with my friends who continue to stand by me no matter what. Sunflowers taught me how to have fun again and how to make life meaningful. Tending to the sunflowers gave my life purpose and meaning when my family left me with a quiet, lonely, empty nest.

This book contains the lessons I learned during this period of growth in my life. The first lesson I learned from the sunflowers was the sun always comes back no matter how bad the storm. The lessons are presented here in the form of seeds of wisdom. I became aware of what I was sowing each day in my life by my actions and words. These lessons created a small movement among my friends called the *Sunflower Principle*. It is a simple guide for living, with all people, regardless of race, religion, or national origin. It is a call to action, to use our individual powers to make a difference in the world. The movement encourages people to take a stand for decency for the benefit of our children and grandchildren. It encourages people to stand up against violence, vulgar language, and nudity, and to hold media companies accountable for their role in the destruction of family values.

By sowing seeds of compassion, love, peace, and understanding, we have the individual power to change our world. My hope is that regular salt-of-the-earth people soccer moms and dads, grandmothers and grandfathers, waitresses, housekeepers, executives, managers, clerks, aunts, sisters, brothers, and cousins will use their voices and their personal influence to call attention to the things about which they are passionate. One's passion may be for inner-city children while another's may be the treatment of the elderly. None of us can single-handedly change the world, but I believe each person has the power to influence others and effect change one person at a time in our small part of the world, thus making it a better place in which to live.

Another purpose of this book is to help the reader recognize the "sunflower" people in their own lives—those who make a difference by the way they live. Once we become aware, we will find sunflower people everywhere who inspire us to live better and become better citizens of our planet.

For lo, the winter is past,
The rain is over and gone.
The flowers appear on the earth,
The time of singing has come,
And the voice of the turtledove
Is heard in our land.
(Song of Solomon 2:11–13, NKJV)

LIFE AFTER DIVORCE

My daughter Robbye loved to plant flowers and dig in the dirt as a little girl. She must have inherited that talent and love of gardening from her grandparents who were experts in the art of growing flower and vegetable gardens and fruit trees. Turning the soil and planting seeds were part of an annual experience when she visited her grandparents in rural Arkansas.

During Robbye's last year at home before going away to college, she planted sunflower seeds in our backyard along the wooden fence next to the gate leading out to the driveway. Tiny green shoots soon broke through the hard, clay soil. With Robbye's love and attention, they quickly grew taller than the eight foot wooden fence. The first blooms brought her such joy. The smile on her face was as bold and beautiful as the sunflowers themselves. An avid photographer, Robbye took many photos of the blooming giants that summer. They became a favorite backdrop for taking pictures of her friends. One particular photograph was a close-up of the golden-brown center of the flower. The detail was magnificent! We had the picture enlarged, matted with a green border, and framed for her room.

I had no idea that those bold, beautiful sunflowers would become as meaningful to me as our family disintegrated. Robbye drove away from home in her cute, little, red convertible, with her golden-blond hair blowing in the breeze. It was her freshman year at Texas Tech. Her big brother Chris was away attending Arkansas State University. I missed him and our long, philosophical conversations.

Divorce ripped our family apart. I acquired the family home, it was a lonely place without the people and activities that once filled it. The quietness of an empty house was truly more than I could bear. Add symptoms of menopause to the loss of my family, and I became one miserable woman.

One morning as I passed through the back gate, one of Robbye's sunflowers almost seemed to turn its head in the breeze and smile at me. "Oh my, you look bright and happy today," I said. As I remember, the sunflower actually responded! Yes, right then, in my sad, emotional state, it is possible I could have qualified for a straitjacket in a padded room. It was a terrible time. I was devastated. Life as I had known it for twenty-five years was shattered into thousands of pieces of glass. My children were angered by the divorce. They stayed away. They wanted no part of the process, and they certainly did not want to take sides.

Being alone, I found I would talk to myself a lot. But anyone who lives alone knows it is not uncommon to talk to oneself, so talking to a flower seemed quite normal to me. In fact, I read somewhere that talking to plants can be therapeutic for them, I found that talking to sunflowers was therapeutic for me.

The long days turned into weeks as the scorching-hot, Texas sun beat down on the sunflowers. With a little water from the garden hose, they grew taller and bolder in color. I was intrigued as they took in my conversation, a spray of water here and there, and the morning sun. I noticed they enjoyed the sunrise as much as I did. They were the only friends I had that were willing to wake up and visit with me at four-thirty or five in the morning. Their droopy, sleepy heads awoke ready to seize the day! Their lovely, dark-brown centers faced the morning sun in the east. In the evenings, they turned their faces to the west and took in the searing rays that deepened their hue. I remember thinking, *what amazing plants these sunflowers are*! They provided food and shelter for a variety of colorful birds. Taking care of the sunflowers and watching the birds became a daily part of my healing process.

It was interesting to me that no matter how hard the rain or how gusty the wind, the flowers stood tall and faced the sun whenever it peeked out from behind the clouds. I couldn't help but think how my own life appeared so much better when I turned toward the light instead of wallowing in the darkness of self-pity. Sunflowers brought a smile to my face and purpose to my life. They were just the "medicine" I needed.

As a mother, I needed something or someone to care for. That had been my life's work. It was a simple pleasure to tend the flowers and watch them grow. My reward was to enjoy the big, beautiful bouquet centered on our Wedgewood-blue breakfast table. I had always said, "If I were rich, I would have fresh flowers in my home every single day." These simple sunflowers were a pot of gold to my soul. I found true wealth in an unexpected source in my own backyard. Loving and caring for the flowers gave me purpose and helped me regain peace of mind.

Lesson 1:
No matter how bad the storm, the sun always comes back.

CHAPTER 2

THE STRANGER AT LUNCH

My friend Keith a woman I worked with at the phone company, and I decided to take our lunch outdoors since it was such a beautiful day. Keith tossed bread crumbs in an arc, high into the air. Hundreds of birds quickly bombed our table. We laughed as we shooed them away. "Keith, you have the heart of St. Francis of Assisi when it comes to tending to God's creatures," I said with a giggle. Her face lit up with pleasure just thinking about the comparison.

Suddenly, a pungent odor pierced our nostrils. We looked up from the table. There in a soiled, gray-striped hospital gown hanging down over what looked like someone else's dirty, khaki pants was an elderly man. Pants unzipped. No belt. The cuffs dragged on the ground. His matted, gray hair hung down to his shoulders. His beard came to a point just at the top of his chest. Then our eyes met. Pure kindness radiated from his deep-set, crystal-clear, blue eyes. His glance was pleading. He spoke volumes, though he said not a word as he reached out his hand, wanting something to eat.

A security guard, in his police blues, came up in a rush. It was against our company's policy for people to panhandle on corporate property. The guard raised his hands, as if trying to scare him away from our table. "Out, get out!" he yelled. We were frightened, at first by the man and then by his treatment. We were as speechless as two marble statues in a courtyard.

At that time, the city of Dallas had just passed an ordinance against giving handouts to the homeless. The hope was that the multitudes who gathered nightly under the bridge would go elsewhere. There were still many who stayed. And there were many who, even under the threat of a fine, still stopped to help.

Neither Keith nor I budged as the guard escorted the old man off the property. His feet shuffled like sandpaper on the concrete patio as he moved slowly along. Our thirty-minute lunch break was over. We headed back to our office, confused and bewildered. The memory haunted us. *Who was that man? Where did he come from? Did he escape from a hospital? Was he someone's father or brother?* Questions flooded our minds for the rest of the day. We were useless on the job. Twenty-one stories up, we stared out the window, hoping to catch a glance of the old man once again. We felt guilty. The scene played out in our minds over and over again. What should we have done? Should we have obeyed the law? Should we have stood up against the authorities? We made a vow to take some type of positive action if anything like that ever happened to us again.

At home that evening, I went into the yard to water the plants. I noticed that several birds would land on the sunflowers' brown centers and peck the seeds allowing them to fall to the ground. They would swoop down and scoop up the seed in their beaks and land on the fence post to savor their find. The cardinals with their bright red jackets were fascinating to watch. I thought about the generosity of these magnificent flowers. They give back through their oil and the foodstuffs they produce for people, wild animals, and birds. They are so much like people, they come in all sizes and colors. They face storms, drought, and other hardships, but no matter what happens, they remain bold and resilient. They hold their heads high and face the sun with confidence. I stopped in my tracks as the vision of the old man returned to my mind.

It is easy for me to show compassion toward my wilting flowers when they need attention. I want them to live and to thrive. And Keith always showed compassion toward birds, dogs, cats, and other animals.

We both shed bitter tears for an old man who may not have found compassion from anyone that day. Some images from our lives stay with us forever. For me, the stranger at lunch is one of them.

Later that evening, I removed a wilted sunflower from the arrangement on my table. And again, the wilted old man returned to my thoughts. I wished I could have been more like the sunflower. I should have been bold, offered my food, and found real help for this helpless old man.

Lesson 2:
Be bold and stand tall with confidence.

CHAPTER 3

SUNFLOWERS, A GIFT OF LOVE

The next summer my sunflower crop was overly abundant. I had more than enough to share. If there was an occasion to give flowers, it was sunflowers that I sent. They became my signature gift.

My friends have received sunflower seeds to plant along with sunflower birthday cards or get well cards. Often I would include a snack of shelled sunflower seeds to munch on as my gift to someone ill or in the hospital. Today, if someone who knows me well thinks of me, she would likely be reminded of the love I have for sunflowers. That is a powerful thing since most of us tend to remember only the negative aspects of a person's life. I am glad that sunflowers have become synonymous with my name.

I gave seeds to Keith who planted them in her backyard next to a high, rock-and-concrete retaining wall. The first year, the gardener cut them down thinking they were weeds. She had enough Mammoth Sunflower seeds left over from the large package I had given her the previous year to plant again in a safe place the following year. As they began to grow, she dared the gardener to whack them down.

It was so much fun to hear Keith's enthusiasm as she told me about each stage of the sunflowers' growth. She, too, had fallen in love with these fabulous "fun flowers." Soon Keith's photos of sunflowers were showing up weekly in my e-mail inbox. *What is the magic these flowers hold which makes people want to capture them in print?*

Before long I had to make the trip out to the ranch where Keith lived to see them for myself. Mammoth was certainly the correct name for these sunflowers. They had grown as tall as the rooftop of her house, and the blossoms were wider than her face. What fun!

As the years passed, I sent sunflower seeds to sunny California for my now grown daughter to plant in the garden of her new home. Her teenage love for these amazing flowers has now come full circle. What she started in our backyard with a few seeds turned out to be like throwing a pebble into a lake and watching the ripples reverberate in every direction. She gave me the gift of love for sunflowers, and they have become my personal expression of love.

Lesson 3:
Love is a boomerang.
Give it away and it will come back to you.

CHAPTER 4

SUNFLOWER FRIENDS

Sri is a beautiful petite woman from India, with shiny black hair down to her waist. Her smile and spirit are inviting to everyone she meets. We became acquainted during a home-study course offered through our church. We would often meet at a nearby park in the mornings and walk together for exercise. We shared many interesting stories about our lives even though they were a world apart. We shared and celebrated the similarities of our faith. Getting to know her through our morning walks was sheer pleasure. Her life growing up in India was certainly a major contrast from my upbringing in rural Arkansas.

Sri was the daughter of a Baptist minister near New Delhi. Because of the important work that her father did, Sri met many wonderful people in her life including Mother Teresa and Billy Graham. Needless to say, I was impressed and was eager to listen to her fascinating stories.

Sri's mother died when she was a little girl which made me feel like a mother figure to her, since I am much older than she. An unlikely pair, we were truly connected by our similar beliefs and an unquenchable sense of adventure. As brave as I think I am, I don't know if I would have been brave enough to leave my country and move to a foreign land as a young woman like Sri had done.

I was also amazed at how much more Sri knew about our country than this Arkansas gal. I listened as she told her stories and shared her hopes and dreams, and she listened to mine. We encouraged each other to follow the desires of our hearts as we grew to become great friends.

Sri and I shared the same sense of compassion for helping others. It was a joint pleasure to lift others up and encourage them to be their best. In one case in particular, Sri assisted me in helping a homeless woman with two cats and no one to turn to. She had lost her job and had been evicted from her apartment. Her personal belongings were scattered all over the grounds of the complex where she had lived. She had been staying in her car until it broke down. Another dear friend, Shirley, took the lady into her home for a few days, but with the woman's cats and Shirley's dog, it was more than she and her husband could tolerate.

Since I was single and alone in a three-bedroom house, I decided to offer her a place to stay. Within three weeks, however, I knew this situation was more than I was equipped to handle. I became her advocate as I tried to help her find housing. While helping her, I also served as her advocate with the Internal Revenue Service (IRS), which was a stretch, even for me. However, I learned that if we can communicate, we can do a lot to change our circumstances. Together, we were able to negotiate an extension that allowed the lady time to get a job before having to pay anything to the IRS.

We spent hours searching all the big job boards on the Internet looking for work she could do. We created an impressive, new résumé for her job search, but we could not penetrate the fear that paralyzed her.

I understood that fear. I had been afraid of starting over. I had been afraid of being alone. One day, as I looked around my house, I noticed all the elephants that I had collected over the years. It dawned on me how much I am like my beloved elephants. Oh, maybe not in size, but in their way of being. It is interesting that an elephant with all of its strength and force can be held back by a small chain on a stake in the ground. That's me, sometimes. I know I have power, strength, gifts, and talents, but I am often held back by the chain of fear and the stake of insecurity. I looked at my new friend and noticed how much she and I were alike. We wanted to change our circumstances, but the fear of something worse than what we had already been through held us hostage. I continued to help her, and in doing so, I noticed that I was breaking free from some of my own chains.

For each job possibility I suggested to her, she had excuses why it would not work. I saw solutions. She could not see beyond her present circumstances.

Thankfully, a neighbor had rescued many of the woman's belongings from the curb and stored them in her own garage. Sri came over to help us move the lady's things into a ministorage facility to keep them safe. We continued to call various shelters for help. They were willing to take her, but not her two cats, which she considered her children. She was determined to keep her "kids." It was so sad. At that moment in her life, the cats seemed to be all the love she had in the world. She would not abandon her cats even at the risk of homelessness.

As hard as we tried, the living arrangements did not work out as I had hoped. I felt she needed emotional help from a professional with skills beyond my abilities. She had taken a beating from life. As a former cover girl and New York model in her youth, the occupation had not given her the security she needed in her later years. She was smart, outgoing, and creative, but she had little knowledge of computers, which is a must in today's world. Most of all, she needed to believe in herself again.

We finally found an extended-stay hotel that would take her and the cats. I paid for a few days' expenses and wished her well, and over time she found others to help her with expenses until she found a job. A few months passed, and I was happy when I heard from her. She had moved into a new apartment and invited me over for a visit. She was on her way to making it on her own once again.

I opened an e-mail from Sri one morning after this important episode. It was the loveliest note I have ever received. It read, "Donna, you are just like a sunflower in the lives of others ... big, bold, and beautiful. Just like a sunflower, you brighten the day of others by all that you do."

Wow! That was quite a compliment. Sunflowers had been my teachers when I was lonely, and now they taught me a new lesson. I could become a sunflower in the lives of other people too. It all started with compassion. It didn't cost a thing to make a difference, and it gave me another reason for living.

Maybe it was just the mothering instinct in me, but I knew for sure that I was born to love, to give, and to serve—that's what all good mothers do. These qualities can take us a long way in our quest for happiness. I found that operating in this purposeful way was to experience time standing still. While helping others, one could spend a whole day without feeling tired, being lonely, or being bored. Being lonely left me watching the clock, but being purposeful or "in-spirit" gave me a burst of energy so I could keep going long after the day ended.

I had stumbled on a simple truth. Just like sowing a few sunflower seeds in my backyard, we humans have opportunities to sow seeds into the life of another every day of our lives. It doesn't take a great education, a lot of money, or personal status. It does take a little bit of time—the best gift we can give. Just like planting seeds in a garden, the reward for planting seeds into the life of another is the abundant harvest of friendship that follows.

Lesson 4:
People can be sunflowers, too.

CHAPTER 5

PRINCIPLE TO LIVE BY

E ver since Sri gave me the gift of becoming a sunflower, I began to see sunflowers everywhere. It's sort of like what some call the "Yellow Volkswagen Theory." For me, the theory could be called the "Red Thunderbird Convertible Theory" because the moment I saw the 1956 T-Bird makeover, I wanted to buy one. At first, there were hardly any around and I wanted something fun and unique. Then I started seeing red Thunderbird convertibles everywhere. That's how it is with sunflowers when you catch the spirit.

Sunflowers show up in life almost every day in some form or fashion. Even if they are out of season, a picture of a sunflower will be the focal point on a book cover, the print of a fabric in a store, an arrangement of artificial flowers, or an advertisement in a magazine. If we look really closely, somewhere there is one tattooed on the arm of a big, burly Harley rider, reminding us of the true meaning of our life's purpose: to be a sunflower in the lives of others.

In order to become a sunflower it is necessary to sow some seeds ourselves—seeds like compassion, love, peace, and understanding. The result of sowing these four tiny seeds can make a difference in our lives, and it might even become the catalyst for change in our world. The movement has started, at least among my closest of friends. I call it the Sunflower Principle. It is a simple concept really. Like the invention of the electric light bulb, I believe it is possible to light up the life of at least one other person.

After becoming aware of the Sunflower Principle, my friend, Linda, and her daughter, Lindsey, returned from a fabulous trip to Prague. There they found a lovely ceramic sunflower and brought it back to me to hang in my window. I was thrilled that they were even thinking of me while on their adventure in another part of the world. Through knowing me, they had become aware of sunflowers everywhere. Their thoughtful gift was a reminder that just as a smile or a tear is universally understood, so, too, is a sunflower recognizable around the globe. The commonalities shared across the globe are truly amazing, and I'm glad sunflowers are among them.

My niece De Anna was in training for a marathon when she visited Dallas from Memphis. She found a walking path not far from my home that I didn't know existed even though I had lived here for thirty years. In order to spend some alone-time with her, I laced up my walking shoes and joined her on the first mile of her walk.

We were walking side-by-side talking as we moved along the trail. I was looking at her and she at me, when in unison we both said, "Oh look, there's a sunflower!" There on either side of the path were wild sunflowers standing tall and greeting us on our way. We both laughed out loud! Just becoming aware of sunflowers is powerful. Once the secret is out you will see them everywhere.

Lesson 5:
The Sunflower Principle is a code of conduct.

CHAPTER 6

SUNFLOWER PEOPLE

If you believe there are sunflower people in the world, they will show up. If you are in trouble, they will come. If you are sad and lonely they will pop up. If you need a new friend and you believe, you will be amazed at what true friendships will develop.

A sunflower person is someone who brings a smile to the face of another. Sunflowers cross the gender gap. Men and women alike can live this principle. He or she lifts others up when they are down. A sunflower person encourages others to live their best life and helps others find their way, even when it seems impossible. He or she sows seeds of peace, love, compassion, and understanding into the lives of others. A sunflower person lives with optimism. Sunflower people look for the best in others without judgment of their actions, mistakes, or their predicaments. They come into our lives without condemnation and they offer unconditional love.

You may find sunflower people in the most unexpected places. When you truly are in need they can show up as angels on earth. If you look, you will find them at any place or at any time, and they will become very important people in your life. The whole concept starts with belief. Believe that you have the power to influence the life of another. Believe that when you need it, someone will show up for you. Just believe!

Almost all people can recall a time when someone influenced their own life by throwing out a proverbial life-line when they were in need. Maybe it was a parent, a relative, a friend, or even a stranger, but in the moment when there seemed to be no way forward, a regular person in the form of an angel showed up in the nick of time. He or she may have offered words of wisdom, a helping hand, or the solution to a problem which seemed so distant that just the idea of it seemed impossible. These unlikely angels are what I call sunflower people. They live their lives by the Sunflower Principle. They make amazing friends. And we can never have too many friends, especially girlfriends.

Friends come in all sizes, shapes, age, and talents. They will stand by you even if the man of your dreams has walked out of your life. They will be there when the kids are grown and on their own. They will walk with you through the dark days of losing parents and friends. Friends are the glue that holds you and me together when everything else in life seems to fall apart.

Lesson 6:
If the best things in life are free—
true friendships must be priceless!

CHAPTER 7

NEW SUNFLOWER FRIENDS

Several years ago a new friend came into my circle. Hylah is as unique as her name. She is bright, fun, and amazingly energetic for her now seventy years of age. She has more self-confidence than anyone I have ever known. Just as I heard her say so often when she talked about her father, she too is a "cockeyed optimist!" Hylah is truly a delight to be around. She always lifts my spirits and encourages me to look on the bright side of everything. She helped me understand what it was like to have a sunflower friend of my own.

Like the gift I had received in the e-mail from Sri, I sent Hylah an e-mail stating that she shows up like a sunflower in my life, big (but not too big), bold, and beautiful, just like a shining sunflower. She absolutely loved the idea, just as much as I had.

From then on, Hylah sent me sunflower cards on special occasions or for no occasion at all, just to let me know she was thinking of me. During one particular sad event in my life, she found a box of Kleenex for me in a bright sunflower pattern. What a difference that small gesture made. Hylah became my cheerleader, confidante, and close friend. She lives up to her reputation of being a sunflower to many other people in her life, too. One can only imagine the number of seeds she has planted in Texas, or perhaps around the world.

Besides being a sunflower to me, Hylah has her own band of followers. It's called The Good Egg Club. This group of amazing women meets for brunch every Sunday after church. Most "Good Eggs" are now grandmothers. Our youngest member, whom we call Jen-Jen, keeps us fresh. She had her first baby in 2010, and now baby Ella has more doting grandmothers than anyone else in the world. She represents a whole new generation of The Good Egg Club.

I have been a "Good Egg" for about nine years now. I'm sure that a decade ago Hylah had no plans to form a long-standing club when she and a friend met at a restaurant called The Good Egg in Dallas. Although the restaurant has since gone out of business, this group of a dozen good friends continues to meet regularly today.

Some observers might say that we eggs are a little cracked. Most of the time when we are together there is a lot of laughter. We have all been hammered by life in some way, but one thing is certain: this beautiful package of a dozen eggs certainly knows how to have fun.

We come from different backgrounds, countries, and races, we attend different places of worship, and we have different interests and talents. One thing this group shares is our faith. We also share each other's joys and sorrows. We encourage and lift up one another. There is no agenda when we meet except to share compassion, joy, unconditional love, and understanding. What a concept! They are all Sunflowers.

Today, Hylah, the founder of The Good Egg Club and the boldest of sunflowers, is fighting the battle of her life as she deals with the devastation of cancer and its treatments. Each week she sends out her newsletter called *"On the Road to a Miracle"* to all of her friends. She states the hard facts and offers words of hope and encouragement to each of us.

Hylah's positivity continues to shine as she sows seeds of love and compassion from her hospital bed. For those Hylah has met during chemo treatments or at the shop where wigs are sold, or in the many doctor's offices she visits, she continues to shine like the bright, bold sunflower person she is. She knows the name of the woman who empties her trash cans and mops her floors. She greets the doctors and nurses with unwavering joy and enthusiasm. There is no doubt about it—Hylah is truly a sunflower to everyone she meets!

Pat, one of my newest Arkansas friends, recently met Hylah for the very first time. She said, "I do not have words to describe this outgoing, vibrant lady." She continued, "Hylah is larger than life!" Pat's assessment of Hylah is true, even though Hylah is operating at only about fifty percent of her regular energy level. Her amazing light continues to brighten any room. To know her is to love her. To be her friend is to have wealth beyond words. While we don't know the outcome of Hylah's battle with cancer, we do know that Hylah has lived well and made a difference with her life. Her joy and enthusiasm are contagious. The character traits of this beautiful sunflower lady will live on in each person who knows her long after her petals have faded. Hylah is considered a sunflower by all of the Good Eggs.

Hylah has three grandsons whom she raves about and longs to be with, but they live in Florida. When she was not able to be with her own grandsons, she virtually adopted children from every walk of life. She has mentored young children like Marion in their faith walk. A beautiful, Brazilian Good Egg named Jaira and her husband are far from their home country. Hylah adopted the couple and their two children and became their American grandmother. She did not take this role lightly. She invited the children over for Easter egg hunts, Halloween parties, or just for the adventure of reading her copy of *Where the Wild Things Are.*

Going to Hylah's house is an instant party, she creates elaborate signs for the front door greeting her guests to make them feel special. She sets a table lavish enough for a queen even if you are just dropping by for coffee. No wonder children everywhere want to go to Hylah's, even us big kids. Her grandchildren say, "Going to Grammy's is like going to Disneyland!" Believe me, it feels that way for us older folks too.

Hylah has served as an usher/greeter at her church for over thirty years. She greets people at the front door all smiles and a genuine interest in anyone new. If she happens to greet a woman who seems to be alone, it is not uncommon for Hylah to invite her to lunch with The Good Eggs. The reward for the Eggs is that we gain a new friend through

Hylah's boldness. She is outrageously friendly, always optimistic, and never uses the words "I'm tired" in conversation. What discipline she has!

Before her hospitalization on Thanksgiving Day, you would find Hylah feeding the homeless in downtown Dallas. She is called the "Pie Lady" by her newly found friends. In my bouquet of friendships, Hylah is the perfect example of what it means to be a sunflower. She keeps her face to the *Son* and she knows the sun will always return. With her love for others and the gifts and talents she openly shares, she is the charter member of the growing movement called the Sunflower Principle. Can you catch the spirit?

Lesson 7:
"Keep your face to the sun and you cannot see the shadows."
—Helen Keller

CHAPTER 8

FRIENDS ARE LIKE FLOWERS

Our world is filled with as many varieties of flowers as it is types of people. Have you ever looked at a person and thought that they resembled a particular flower? If you haven't before, you will, going forward.

My dear friend, Elaine, and I share November birthdays. One year I found the perfect card to give her. It read, "Friends are like flowers." How true that is. All of the friends in this particular group differ in size, personality, and interests, but we are beautiful, like a big bouquet of flowers, when we all come together. This group calls itself the WOW Group. Originally this acronym stood for Wise Older Women, however, as we have all aged, many did not like being called older so the name was changed to Wild Outrageous Women. Either way, this group has one main agenda, which is to have fun.

Some WOW's are successful in business, some have amazing leadership abilities, some are bright, fun, and outgoing, and some have incredible senses of humor, like Pat. This forever-young lady is in her seventies. She runs circles around the rest of us, offering wisdom about diet and exercise and the value of holistic medicine for a healthy, long life. She is a perpetual student of life, health, and wellness.

Pat loves to share a good joke and she is the first one to arrive when someone is in need. All of the ladies in the WOW group are intelligent, loving, caring, and giving, including two or three husbands who participate from time to time. The WOW's come from different places, different walks of life and practice different faiths. They all bring with them the gifts of friendship and love. I consider each of them and The Good Egg Club to be powerful sunflower friends.

Like me, Elaine is an Arkansas girl. She is the founder of the WOW group. We instantly had a lot in common from our rural upbringing. We had to wait nearly forty years to meet in Texas, but our Arkansas roots made us fast and lasting friends.

We enjoy using words and phrases that the others in our group do not understand. Southern phrases like, "I swan," which actually means "I swear." Instead of swearing, ladies would draw out the word swan like, suh-waaaahn. No self-respecting belle from the South would ever swear. We relish the fun days of Arkansas living where times were often hard, but where children learned to entertain themselves by catching crawdads or lightning bugs. It was a good life for children that left us with fond memories and good values. Weeping willow trees were abundant and their branches were used to correct bad behavior. Talking back to an adult was unheard of if a child wanted to live to be twenty. Parents were respected as were all adults. Work and responsibility were taught just like *readin'* and *writin'*. An education consisted of more than what was taught at school. If students misbehaved at school, they were sure to be in trouble when they got home. We are truly grateful for having lived during this period in history.

Elaine has many gifts. She is exceptional at introductions and match making and is the ultimate party giver and event planner. She never forgets a birthday. After we celebrated her birthday with all of our friends, she gave me an exquisite party just a few days later in the private dining room of the lovely May Dragon Chinese Restaurant. I requested that no one bring gifts, but instead I wanted everyone to bring a single flower that represented their own personality and style.

One-by-one, more than twenty friends arrived carrying an assortment of flowers. Some, like Shirley, Weldon, and their daughter, brought in a big bouquet of various colored carnations. "We found it difficult to buy just one flower," Shirley said. I laughed as I thought how appropriate it was since Shirley wears so many different hats in all of her varied interests. The whole bouquet was certainly appropriate for this busy lady.

Hylah naturally showed up with a big, bright, beautiful sunflower, which certainly did not surprise me. Marcela, a beautiful Latina, brought in the most perfect red rose that was so her. Elaine presented me with a bird of paradise—unique, bright, colorful and fun, just as she is. Each friend presented me with her flower and told her own story of what the flower meant to her. Sherri never ceases to amaze me. She is one of our most creative friends. She made a bouquet of ink pens wrapped in floral tape with little silk flowers hot glued to the top. What a treat that gift was even after all the live flowers were gone.

That birthday party was truly a beautiful experience. The whole event was more enjoyable than I could have imagined, as each person told about her flower and the relationships we had built over time.

By the end of the evening, I had the most gorgeous and amazing bouquet I had ever received in my life. Just as the party was coming to a close, Isabella came in with a single stem of live orchids. They were a beautiful addition to the bouquet. Everyone oohed and aahed! It was just like Isabella. She is a unique person and world traveler. Her beautiful smile acts like a magnet, drawing people in no matter where she goes. She has so many interesting stories to tell from her exotic trips, the orchids certainly reflected her personality perfectly.

For the next two weeks I smiled at the flowers and admired the enormous bouquet that graced my dining room table. There were fragrant roses and carnations of every color, there were unusual flowers whose names I don't know even today. All were truly unique and beautiful, just like my friends. It was a bouquet of many colors. Some of them were bright purple, others orange, there were yellow and white daisies, and various colors of lilies and roses.

Several other good friends who were unable to attend the party blessed me with lovely cards and e-mail messages. Their sentiments remained within the special theme of flowers and friendship. Their lovely written messages were truly worthy of publication and sharing with the world. I was so touched!

Cards can be expensive today, so I make sure I enjoy them as long as possible. My birthday is November 15th. I display my birthday cards on the fireplace mantle until Christmas cards begin to arrive. Then when I take down the birthday cards, I reread them. I realize how blessed I am to have such loving, caring people in my life.

One-by-one the flowers withered, drooped, faded, and dried up. I removed them from the vase as they died. To me that seemed to represent our own lives as we bloom for a while here on earth before passing on to the heavenly dimension of eternal life. What we leave behind depends on the kinds of seeds we have sown.

I was amazed that after more than two weeks the last flower standing was the delicate stem of orchids. I moved it into a bud vase all by itself, and I realized how special it was that it was the last bloom to arrive at the party and the last one to die and go away. I would never have guessed that the most delicate would also have the most endurance. I couldn't help but think about how precious the lives of our friends are to us. Some come into our life and stay for a lifetime and others pass through, sow their seeds of wisdom, and move on.

Sadly, just a few months after that fabulous birthday party, Nan my oldest and boldest of friends passed away suddenly. It was truly a shock! With her fighting spirit, I thought she would outlive many of us. But it was not to be. Nan was an artist who loved color. When she put on her makeup in the mornings, her face was radiant like it had been airbrushed for a fashion magazine. Her face was her canvas and she used color to bring out her best features.

Before Nan's passing, she gave to the world several paintings in oil and watercolor. When she described things, she spoke of them as being happy. Happy was her favorite word. I'm thrilled to know that she had enjoyed one of my little gifts of sunflower seeds that I had sent with a card for her birthday the year before. She loved them. She told me how much fun she had planting the happy sunflowers in her yard. The flowers bloomed as boldly as Nan had lived.

We are not promised a long, healthy, vibrant life. However, we can make the life we do have special and meaningful, one dayat a time. We know there may not be a tomorrow for us, but we all have today to live and sow the seeds outlined in *The Sunflower Principle.*

Lesson 8:
"To everything there is a season, a time for every purpose under heaven, a time to be born, and a time to die, a time to plant, and a time to pluck what is planted."
(Ecclesiastes 3:1-2, NKJV)

CHAPTER 9

A SEED OF COMPASSION

All of us, no matter our station in life, our financial situation, or our relationship to our community, have seeds of greatness within us, just waiting to be shared. There are people hurting everywhere just waiting for someone to care. There are people who are lonely everywhere. There are people who would like to share their story if they had someone with a listening ear. We must make an effort to bloom wherever we are planted. In order to do so, we have to get out and plant a few seeds of our own.

It is easy to focus on our own pain and the losses in our lives. When we stay focused on our personal issues, we tend to live with worry, fear, and loneliness instead of making a difference in the world and healing our own hurts at the same time.

We live in a society today that has a pill for every ailment. We have canned drinks to give us energy, along with coffee and tea to get us going in the mornings. All these things may help, but stepping out of ourselves is better than any of the popular energy boosters sold over the counter. Why would we not want to feel good when there is a simple solution? I have found that when I go out to help someone else I instantly feel better.

As we go about our day, we are constantly scattering seeds. What we get in return depends on what we have sown. When we complain about how bad things seem, we find more of the same. When we see the beauty in others, our outlook grows much brighter. We can bring sunshine into the life of another or we can be the cloud of doom and gloom.

We must first have a seed of compassion to get along well in this life. We can't go through life like a horse with blinders on and ignore all that is going on around us. There are people hurting everywhere. To a person who is lonely, a smile and simple "hello" is a welcome gift. For someone who is depressed, a cure can be found in a pair of listening ears. For someone who has grown older and feels forgotten, a few moments of our time are priceless.

It is easier to have compassion for the homeless and for people who have experienced tragic losses. But when it comes to those closest to us, we often judge and criticize, especially those we know well. We observe their lives and know about the choices they have made. We know that their lives could have been different, "if only …." So, we often find ourselves sending money to those causes which are more immediately deserving like television ministries, or other worthy causes, when in fact there are persons in our own families who are hurting and suffering. Gifts of money may not be the solution for their problems. Perhaps all they really need is a restored relationship that was taken away many years before.

How often have children experienced the loss of a parent after divorce? One parent goes off and marries someone else, beginning a new, separate life. Often they become the parents and caregivers to someone else's children because it is easier than trying to be the weekend "Disneyland Dad" to their own.

This happened in my own life when my dad married a woman who had three sons. They were married for over twenty years. My brother and I were never invited to a family holiday meal at their home. When I asked my dad, "What are you doing for Christmas or for the weekend?"

He would often say, "Oh, the kids are coming over."

I wanted to scream! "What am I, if not your child?"

Dad was much older than his new wife. The plan was that he would die before her and everything they had worked for would become hers. It was not to be. She died. "The kids" showed my dad their loyalty for all the years he helped provide for them. They wanted everything, the house, the car, the antiques, the keepsakes. So they took it, not that the estate was significant enough to fight over. The inheritance my brother and I received was priceless. We got our dad back. Even after all those years, I learned that it is never too late to have a father, even if he only shows up again in his 80's.

With compassion we can welcome home a prodigal son or father. With a small seed of compassion we can change our very own world. Sometimes that means we must also have a little compassion for ourselves.

Lesson 9:
The first seed for living the Sunflower Principle is *compassion*.

LOVE IN ACTION

A s grandmothers it is easy for us to hold our first-born grandchild and fall head over heels in love with the tiny soul who is a part of us. I felt that kind of love when I held my grandson, Peter, for the very first time. It was love at first sight, he holds a very special place in my heart today and always. It was easy to love him, he is flesh of my flesh. My love for him is immeasurable. At birth, he looked just like his handsome dad, Chris. How could I not love him? Peter lives in England, so I don't get to see him often, but my love for this amazing child is eternal.

It was a couple of years ago though that I discovered what I call instant love. We have instant coffee, instant tea, and today we have instant soft drink dispensers for our homes. There was a period in history when brewing coffee or tea took time. Soft drinks went through the conveyer belts at the bottling company before being delivered to the store. But, today we are thrilled by instant products and cannot wait for the latest one that comes along that promises instant success. Could there be instant love? I had never heard of it before until it happened to me.

Instant love is insane. How big is this crazy instant love? It is easily as large as three times infinity. It is like a superhuman love I have never known. My daughter, Robbye and her husband Scott, had been married almost ten years and had not had any children of their own, so they decided to adopt. The process was unbelievably difficult and time consuming. Finally, they received the call that two children were available for them to pick up. They were brother and sister, the boy was two and the girl was three. We were thrilled beyond belief at the addition to our family. It was just a few days later when the agency called again saying there was another child from the same mother who was just born and placed in foster care. Needless to say they could not separate the baby girl from her siblings. So this free-spirited family of two was instantly changed to a family of five, almost overnight. They were ecstatic!

I was thrilled too, and I could not wait to make the trip to California to see my new grandchildren. It was at first glance that I learned about instant love. Amazing love! Unconditional love! Something changed within me. These beautiful children with their deep brown skin, coal black hair, and sparkly brown eyes had me hook, line, and sinker.

I have learned, however, that love is not always that easy. Sometimes we have to try really hard to love someone. And, I might often be surprised to learn that sometimes I am unlovable at times myself.

I saw love in action through my mother, who never ceases to surprise me with her selfless acts of kindness and generosity. Several years ago, she was driving around town when she noticed a little boy playing by the street. She stopped to talk to him, but he obviously could not hear her, nor could he talk. Worried about the little boy's safety, she knocked on the door of the house to talk with his mother. That one visit, fueled with concern and compassion, changed the life of that child. The lady of the house told my mother that she had been praying for someone who would come along to help her son. She was not well-educated and her financial situation would not allow for the kind of help her son needed. She was older when the boy was born, and as a mother, she worried about what would happen to him after she was gone, since he could not hear or speak.

Over the next few months my mother and her friend Dora took the little boy to a doctor who made appointments with the school for the deaf in Little Rock. The little boy received the medical help and education that he needed to become the successful employee and family man he is today. My mother exhibited unconditional love and compassion for a perfect stranger. I may not remember all the lessons that she tried to teach me while I was growing up, but I will never forget what she did for that little boy.

There are opportunities for making a difference right in our own neighborhoods. We must take off our blinders, get out of the rat race, and really listen with our ears, and see with our eyes and heart in order to know what is going on around us.

Our world today presents many challenges fueled by hatred, prejudice, anger, greed, and the insatiable hunger for power over another. I believe the people of our world are primarily of one race—the race of humanity. We are all one! We are all born in the same way. We all breathe, laugh, cry, eat, live, and die. I believe, however unfortunately, that our society is actually broken down into two sub races, one of hate and the other of love. It doesn't matter what color our skin or what religion we practice, we either love or we hate. We are constantly moving in one direction or the other. We are not born into one of these sub races. We are taught or we choose to which race we belong. The seeds we sow only yield what we plant.

People often speak about their faith, their church affiliation, or the friendships they have formed through their places of worship. Most of the time we worship with people who are of like minds and very similar beliefs. Our places of worship generally reflect more people who look a lot like us. It's true, our faith is central to many of our relationships. To catch the spirit of the Sunflower Principle, however, is to embrace the world and *all* people, everywhere, with understanding and acceptance instead of fear.

One Sunday morning my friend, Beverly (an amazing Good Egg), shared a story of her recent adventure, walking the steps where St. Paul preached in Greece. She showed us pictures of the Parthenon and the Acropolis in Athens. She described how Paul preached from the great mountain tops. One slide had a scripture from Paul's Letter to the Galatians in Chapter 1:28 of *The Good News Bible* by the American Bible

Society. "There is no difference between Jews and Gentiles, between slaves and free men, between men and women. You are all one." This was written around 35 AD.

Although Beverly continued with her slide presentation and her talk, my mind was locked in on the words Paul wrote so long ago. How many times have we heard this, how many times have we read this and why can't we all get it? We are all one. This is not news! Would we deliberately inflict pain and torture on ourselves? We do when we hate our brothers and sisters. What would happen if those of us in the world who really believe that we are all one spoke up and voiced our opinions? We only hear of all the hate and all the war and all the bad in the world. Do we have the power to demand change that fosters love instead of hate? We won't have to wait on global warming or pollution to do us in if we continue to resent and hate others because they look different than we do. We often have an insatiable need to be right. If others disagree with us they must be wrong. If they are wrong, we must be in opposition. If we are on opposing sides and we are so convicted that ours is the only way, we end in war with the result being the bloodshed of our sons and daughters.

On September 11, 2001, our nation stood still as we watched in horror when the Twin Towers exploded before our very eyes. One airplane after another hit the towers as we held our collective breath in disbelief. None of us will ever forget that day.

I had just dropped Chris off at the Dallas/Fort Worth International Airport early on that fateful morning as I was going to work. Chris was returning to his home in New York City. His flight had only been in the air a few hours when all aircraft were ordered to land at the nearest airport. Chris's flight was grounded in Chicago. For that I am eternally grateful. For thousands of others around the world, hearts were broken at the loss and injuries of their loved ones on the planes, in the Twin Towers, and on the ground. That moment in time forever changed us as a nation.

This tragedy, as horrific as it was, made Americans angry and, yet, at the same time we pulled together to show our love and support for one another and for our country. Our bold colors of red, white, and blue were flying all over the country. Decals and flags were attached to our cars and trucks to show support for those who lost their lives and as an expression of the love we have for our country. Men wore American flags on their lapels and women were adorned with jewels of red, white, and blue. Today each time I see my crystal bracelet lying in my jewelry box, it reminds me of what love can do following the pain inflicted on a nation by the forces of hate.

It must have been terrible to be a law-abiding American citizen from the Middle East living in America at the time. People were commonly judged by their skin color and their name. Many people from other countries shared stories of being mistreated because some thought they might be the enemy. While some showed acts of hatred for a single race of people or a religious group, others sought to understand.

My friend Judi is a fascinating woman of Jewish heritage. She formed a group of multicultural people who met weekly mainly to try to understand one another. At first there were only seven or eight people who attended. As the weeks passed our numbers grew. Members represented many religions such as Islam, Judaism, Buddhism, Sikhism, Hinduism, Taoism, and Christianity.

Those weekly gatherings were fascinating and educational. Overall it seemed our brothers and sisters of these foreign faiths were at the core the same as my Christian brothers and sisters. We all agreed on the laws to live by, like the Ten Commandments. We all agreed that the basic laws of living a good life consisted of love for one another and treating others as we want to be treated. Everyone expressed concern over the fact that there are extremists in all faiths.

I found all of the people to be warm, friendly, and caring. I believe that when we take time to know others well, our enemies become our friends. Just as integration changed American society, my hope is that people of different religions will eventually have more opportunities to come together to really get to know one another. I hope to see more international schools and places of worship where children of all cultures can come together and learn to love, respect, and understand one another. There would be myriad benefits including the opportunity to learn another language besides our own.

There are many questions about life and death that I do not attempt to understand, much less try to answer. I do not believe it is up to us to understand all the things we question in this lifetime. Mother Teresa lived a self-sacrificing life. She dedicated her heart and soul to spreading the word of God. She was a devoted servant for Jesus, but even she did not have all the answers. Like many of us, Mother Teresa questioned her faith at times. I read a quote from EWTN Global Catholic Network where Mother Teresa stated, "There is only one God and He is God to all, therefore it is important that everyone is seen as equal before God. I've always said we should help a Hindu become a better Hindu, a Muslim become a better Muslim, a Catholic become a better Catholic. We believe our work should be our example to people." Although there are many who would debate Mother Teresa's philosophy, I am convinced that Mother Teresa served others with the heart of Jesus. Jesus' life is documented in the Gospels as being all inclusive when dealing with the people He met. Jesus is the example for my faith as a Christian. I believe there is one God, and He hears our prayers of forgiveness wherever and whomever we are. He is not concerned about our race or religious affiliation or our social status. I believe God wants His people to be giving, loving and of service to others, no matter who they are, or what they believe. It is certainly not my place to judge anyone for what he or she chooses to believe, but as a Christian it is my place to love them regardless. I would be very concerned about believing in any religion that preached anything less than love.

After meeting with my new friends of various world religions, I began to think that when we are born we must have within our DNA an inherent desire to worship. We do not come with a road map of how to worship, but with a great desire to worship something greater than ourselves. Just like the need to breathe, we seem to need to worship. Perhaps that desire is also the desire to love and be loved just as we are. I must remember what it says in my Bible,…but the greatest of these is love." 1 Corinthians 13:13b (NKJV)

Several years ago I traveled to Rwanda and the Congo with a small group whose job it was to build a school and small medical clinic for the treatment of AIDS in many of the women and children of Rwanda. While there, we visited a small, rural, brick church called Ntarama, just a few miles outside of Kigali. Inside the building, on either side of the door, were several bookcases. Instead of books lined up, as one would expect, there were skulls of people left as a shrine and memorial of the horrible genocide that took place there.

A wildfire of hate and prejudice resulted in nearly five thousand people being slaughtered. There were garbage bags full of skulls of little children that had been raked up and stacked like garbage waiting to be picked up. This scene was forever etched in my mind. It is an awful and extreme example of sowing seeds of hate. What I learned from that visit was this, hate kills and love heals!

Lesson 10:
The second seed is *love*, the forerunner of peace.

Chapter 11

PEACE

B ack in the sixties there were peace signs everywhere. Sunflowers were
painted on the sides of Volkswagens along with the words *peace* and
love. It was a time of war. It was a time of conflict. Anger and resentment
were fueled by the deaths of our young men and women serving in
Vietnam. Everyone wanted peace. "Love-ins" attracted thousands of
young people strumming their guitars and singing songs of peace,
hoping that the world would see that we needed love, not war.

All of us would love to live in a peaceful world, but it is an elusive
dream. The numbers of news reports about war, crime and violence
astronomically outweigh the good news of peace. We are constantly
bombarded with pictures of bloodshed in the Middle East. We send our
children off in the name of peace only to have hundreds flown back to
their families in wheelchairs or wooden boxes.

I believe that mothers everywhere cry in the same heart wrenching
language over the loss of their children. None of us wants to see the
uniformed officers show up at our door, whether we are being notified of
a deadly crime in our city or of landmines blowing up the body of our
son or daughter. Will it ever stop? The answer is probably not, at least
not in my lifetime. But do we have to accept it as if there is nothing we
can do about it? I don't think so.

Back in Texas, in a church I once belonged to, we always ended the
service by holding hands across the aisle and singing what is called "The

Peace Song," written by husband and wife Sy Miller and Jill Jackson. The song was first introduced at the church to a group of multicultural students who were deliberately brought together in hopes of teaching young people how to get along with all races.

The Peace Song says: "Let there be peace on earth and let it begin in me..." The song may not ever fulfill the dreams of world peace, but it certainly makes us stop and think about what action we can take to promote peace by our own words, actions and deeds. If we strive each day to live in peace with our families, our neighbors, our business associates, and others we may encounter, we have begun the process of living by the Sunflower Principle, which promotes planting seeds of peace in all of our relationships. Change actually does begin within each of us.

Lesson 11:
The third seed is *peace*—"Let it begin in me."

CHAPTER 12

UNDERSTANDING

Often we are fearful of others who may look different or speak differently from us. It happened to me one night while living alone in an apartment in Dallas. I normally go to bed early and do not open the door for anyone after dark if they do not call first. On this particular night, it was about eleven o'clock when my doorbell rang several times. Then someone started beating on the door. I grabbed my robe and looked through the peephole in the door, but I couldn't recognize the people there. There were two men. One was older than the other, and he spoke in a language that I had never heard before. The other could speak English and seemed to be much younger. They kept knocking loudly. Finally I heard them as they tried to turn a key in the door. *They are trying to unlock my door*! I silently screamed.

My imagination went wild as I held onto the deadbolt. I heard the younger one say, "She's in there. She has the deadbolt locked!" I ran for the phone and dialed 911 and waited for the police to arrive. I went back to the door and held tight to the deadbolt lock. In a few moments I heard the scuffing of their shoes on the concrete as they walked away.

Soon the officer was at the door. He rang the bell and yelled, "Police." I opened the door. To my surprise the officer removed a note from the door stating that I had left my car keys and house keys in the door, and that my neighbors had my keys in their apartment for safekeeping. I was so embarrassed! I couldn't apologize enough. I felt like such a fool. The officer retrieved my keys and assured both of us that no harm was done. I was up until after four in the morning, thinking about how my kind neighbors had attempted to help and protect me, while my imagination ran wild. I immediately sat down and wrote a letter of apology and sincere thanks for their kindness. I only hoped they would forgive me for calling the police.

In our society today we often think the worst, when actually something good is about to take place. I wondered how often I had missed a blessing because of the stories I made up in my head. I also thought about how rapidly my fear grew although I only had a few of the facts and did not understand what was going on.

We often make quick judgments out of fear about people who appear different. It is not always the fear of the unknown, but it is our lack of understanding and our own imaginations going into overdrive that cause us to resort to fear-based thinking.

Our planet has become so small that we must learn to live with one another in peace, love, compassion, and understanding in order for our world to survive. The people in our town no longer all look the same. We do not all speak the same language. We do not all eat the same foods or attend the same worship, as we did in the past.

In my travels, I have discovered that all people have the same needs for food and shelter. All people have the ability to love and accept another even if they do not share the same faith. Christians, Jews, Muslims, Hindus, or any other religious groups all share a longing for peace and love. Mothers everywhere weep at the loss of their children. People all over the globe laugh out loud. A belly laugh is universally understood. Because we are more alike than different, all of us can embrace this simple principle and join the movement toward a better world. Who knows how one tiny seed or idea could bring people together?

The four seeds outlined in the Sunflower Principle are not unique to any one ethnic group or one religion. Wouldn't it be wonderful if people everywhere were to recognize the sunflower as being a universal symbol for peace, love, compassion, and understanding? It is a bold, ambitious idea! The sunflower is a bold flower, it is able to withstand high winds and perfect storms, and still rise up to face the sun again. The sunflower knows its source. It is sturdy and resilient. It is generous and gives back through oil and seeds for people, animals, and birds to enjoy. Although sunflowers come in different colors and sizes, they are all the same. They are sunflowers!

Lesson 12:
The fourth seed is *understanding*—
the Golden Gate to building relationships.

CHAPTER 13

TEACHERS ARE SUNFLOWER'S IN FULL BLOOM

M y own grandmother was the most influential person in my life. When I was around the age of three or four, my grandmother taught me to sing the little song, *"Jesus Loves the Little Children,"* written by C. Herbert Woolston in the 1800's. As we belted out the words, "… all the children of the world, red, yellow, black, and white, they are precious in His sight …" She gave me the best gift of all. For as long as I can remember I have believed exactly what that song said. Ma, as I called her, planted the seed of love in me which extends to all people. Today because of this wise woman I remain fascinated by the different cultures, customs, and beliefs of people in our world. What do you teach through your words and actions? You may be the catalyst for change in your family, and that is the best place to start.

Children do not come into the world hating. Hate, prejudice, and feelings of superiority over others are learned behaviors. When we are little, the actions of those around us are our greatest teachers. Parents may not intend to teach hate and prejudice, but subtle expressions, words, and actions teach more by accident than many teachers do on purpose.

Right now, wherever you are and no matter how old you are, you have the power to influence at least one other person. Start now to make a list of the people who look up to you. Maybe people come to you with their problems because you are a good listener. Maybe they trust you for giving them the answers they seek. This relationship represents a sphere of influence. Start there. You may have more power of influence than you think.

Unfortunately, many others use their influence to encourage our children and grandchildren to become involved in drugs and violence to the point that many have become desensitized to the value of human life. Many video games our children play teach killing, destruction, and fighting. How can this be considered fun? Who among us will love our children and grandchildren enough to stand up for decency, respect, courage, and honor?

Do you enjoy the vulgar language our little children have learned? Who taught them these words? Who sowed these vulgar seeds? Someone has to take responsibility if we ever want to see change. Will it be you? Will you take a stand for what is being taught to the little children in your town? If the young children in your life were to quote you, would you be proud of the words they used? Children are like little sponges. They soak up every word. For some reason they will remember a swear word and use it long before they speak in sentences.

Once I was asked to try this experiment. My pastor stood up on a chair and asked me to take his hand to see if he could pull me up off the ground. Of course he could not. Then he asked me to take his hand again and see if I could pull him down off the chair. Naturally, that was a much easier task. His point was loud and clear. You can be pulled down to someone else's level easier than you can pull them up to yours. And this is what is happening to our children. They have people pulling them down all the time and if we don't have a strong hold on them they will easily slip out of our hands. Every year and each season of life we lose many of the things that matter. We can't sit by any longer and hope that someone else will take action. While we are waiting for someone else, those with nothing to lose continue to take away many of the rights and privileges we hold dear.

There are many issues and worthy causes to support. One person may not change the world as a whole, but one person can make a difference to many others. One of my favorite old stories is an important reminder of the difference a person can make. It's called "The Starfish Story," a Harvest/HBJ Book of 1979, written by Loren Eiseley, a well-respected essayist, philosopher, and literary naturalist. My retelling has been simplified and modernized from Eiseley's original tale. It goes something like this:

One day a man was walking along the beach when he noticed a boy picking something up and gently throwing it into the ocean. Approaching the boy, he asked, "What are you doing?"

The youth replied, "Throwing starfish back into the ocean. If I don't throw them back, they will die."

"Son," the man laughed, "don't you realize there are miles and miles of beaches and hundreds maybe thousands of starfish? There is no way you can make a difference!"

The boy bent down, picked up another starfish, and threw it back into the waves. Then, with a smile on his face, he looked up at the man and said, "I made a difference for that one."

Whatever we are concerned about in our society today, we can influence the life of another and make a difference one person at a time. Maybe you are concerned about our educational system or gangs in your community, or maybe you know just one person who is having a really difficult time. It could be a single mother with two or three children who could use a night out or a day to do something for herself. Each of us can take action to better the life of someone in these situations. For large issues like the educational system in our country, writing your congressman or congresswoman may be a place to start. Try volunteering for a day or two for a local nonprofit to see for yourself how you can help. For dangerous issues like the presence of gangs, maybe you could organize a youth group, or volunteer for one already in existence. Perhaps you already know some young pre-teen that you can mentor in order to keep him or her from joining a gang. There is always something each of us can do.

Perhaps the warehousing of our elderly in nursing homes is something about which you are passionate. Many people live day-in and day-out with no visitors or anyone who truly cares about them. What can you do? Find one person like this and make an effort to be a friend or an advocate for that person. Visit them, take them a book, a flower, a bookmark, or just give them a hug. This is a way to make a difference just like the boy in the starfish story.

Lesson 13:
If life is a movie and you are the star—
how will you play your staring role?

CHAPTER 14

SEARCHING FOR STARS AMONG THE SUNFLOWERS

All of us in America today have heard of the group known as MADD, Mothers Against Drunk Driving. This non-profit organization was founded thirty years ago by Candy Lightner, whose own daughter was killed by a repeat drunk driving offender. Candy took that terrible tragedy and turned it into something positive by taking action to influence change in the laws that had previously allowed drivers to continue to drive after receiving citations for drunk driving. There is no way to know how many lives she saved by standing up, speaking out, and taking action. Candy Lightner is definitely a superstar!

Often after a great loss like a death, divorce, or a prolonged illness, we feel as if our lives have spun out of control. It seems that we have ended up in a dark tunnel from which we will never escape. It is easy to get depressed. In fact, it is normal. Although one episode of our lives may have ended there is still plenty of life left to live, so live it with purpose and with passion. What are you passionate about? Whatever keeps you awake at night or makes your heart sing during the day, that is your passion. Passion is a call to action for you and me to do something. By taking action our lives become filled with purpose. Our purpose is waiting to be revealed no matter what our age. The following are a few people I know who are over sixty-five years of age who inspire me by the contributions they make at a time when most people are ready to kick back. These ladies are sunflower people and superstars without a doubt.

There is a group of ladies in my church who are lovingly called the Sunday School Ladies. The collective gifts of these women could change the world. They have a heart for service and their lives reflect love and compassion through their many acts of kindness. The more I get to know them individually, I realize what amazing people they truly are.

Cherry Frierson is one of those ladies whom I have grown to admire. Cherry struggled with a learning disability all of her life, long before dyslexia was identified as a spatial shift and reversal in reading patterns. Over the years she learned to compensate for her unnamed disorder and eventually graduated college and became a kindergarten teacher. She learned to identify children who, like her, had trouble learning. She constantly studied and searched for information to help her students. Cherry and her daughter, Mary Margaret, who also is a teacher, decided to start a program called APPLE—an acronym for Alternative Programs Providing Learning Experiences—which supports parents and teachers of dyslexic students. After an interview with Cherry, I found that APPLE was better than the gift of an apple to the teachers. Because of her dedication to improving the learning processes of children who struggled with dyslexia, she was able to develop programs and processes to make a difference in the lives of children like herself and like her son.

Cherry lost her son during the time of building the APPLE Foundation. In her life, like so many others, she has suffered major losses and huge set backs, but this tragic loss only furthered her cause. Cherry is both a superstar and a sunflower person in my book.

Rosalie Barber is another inspiring woman whom I admire for her dedication and selfless acts of service. Rosalie spent thirty-one years as a faculty member at Arkansas State University. Beyond her career, Rosalie is a volunteer manager and buyer for the St. Bernard's Medical Center gift shop. She also volunteers and has served as a member of the National Advisory Council for the Beck PRIDE Center at Arkansas

State University since its inception in 2007 and was recently elected Secretary. The Beck Pride Center (Personal Rehabilitation, Individual Development and Education) was established to assist returning wounded veterans in all areas of their lives. Rosalie says, "Volunteering with PRIDE is the one area of volunteerism that I am particularly proud to be a part of. PRIDE provides assistance in enrolling at ASU, professional counseling, scholarships, financial assistance, etc. Hundreds of wounded veterans have been assisted by this program."

Rosalie is a three time cancer survivor who inspires me to never give up. Her passion and commitment to her church and the community has caused everyone lucky enough to call her friend to burst with pride.

Pat Oplinger and I met in 2011 at the Hemingway-Pfeiffer Creative Writers' Retreat. Pat lives in the foothills of Arkansas. She spent thirty-nine years as an educator in Pennsylvania before moving to Arkansas upon retirement. Pat is an award-winning writer of essays, book reviews, columns, and articles for literary magazines and newspapers. One would think that this busy mother and grandmother would use this time of her life to sit back and do what she loves to do—write. Although, she does do that frequently, what impresses me most about Pat is that she decided to use her skills and knowledge to establish a program called The Storybook Project. It is a literacy program inside prison units which provides the opportunity for male and female inmates to record storybooks on digital voice recorders for their children. Then she and other volunteers mail the books and CD's to the children and grandchildren of the incarcerated. Pat saw a need and now fifteen years later, the project is stronger than ever and will expand shortly to other correctional units in Arkansas.

This is just the beginning of my "star search." Who knows who will be next? When we take the time to really get to know someone we almost always find a superstar waiting to be discovered. It is my hope that these people will inspire each of us to use our skills and talents to make a difference with our lives and expand the theory of the Sunflower Principle. My desire is to be a writer who makes a difference through the things I write. Without the support of friends, I never would have had the courage to pursue this book. But it is because of people like those who have inspired me that I am moving forward with my goals.

My purpose is to sow some good seeds and to encourage others to do the same. Anyone can be a cheerleader for someone else who might be struggling or afraid to move forward. I have never heard anyone tell me that they get too much praise or too many pats on the back. The November 2009 McKinsey Quarterly reported a survey where their respondents preferred praise from their immediate managers more than financial incentives. It's no wonder that appreciation won by a landslide. You can pay anyone to do a job, but appreciation is a gift from the heart. It's priceless! Developing an attitude of gratitude and praise is an easy habit to develop. A gift of a kind word touches the soul of the receiver.

We encounter people everyday that may not have received a kind word of praise in years, if ever. We have the power to sow seeds with our words. Let's take inventory of the seeds we are planting. When they sprout, they are only going to produce more of the same. Sometimes it only takes a word to make a difference!

Lesson 14:
Start each day with an attitude of gratitude—
the reward is more to be thankful for.

CHAPTER 15

JOIN HANDS

This circle of friends started with just one person. Hylah invited one person to lunch one day. The next week she invited another and the story repeated itself over the years until her group of friends numbered in the hundreds. We saw many of them recently at the beautiful memorial service of this amazing sunflower person. Hylah lost her battle with cancer, but she planted so many good seeds into the lives of those who knew her that she continues to live on in our hearts and in our actions.

Hylah encourged me to continue writing the last time I saw her. She handed me a little piece of paper she had cut from an advertisement for Chico's. It read, "Confidence is the single most beautiful thing a woman can wear every day." She went on to say, "Keep this as a reminder that with confidence you can achieve your dreams." So, I am finishing my first book in honor of the best cheerleader in all the world, Hylah McCollum.

Hylah wanted her memorial service to be fun and special. She wanted the congregation to sing songs that we learned as children in Vacation Bible School. The service was a joyous celebration of a life well-lived. She gave the minister detailed instructions on what she wanted her to say. In that service she borowed a line from my book that Hylah had been helping me edit. The minister said, " Keep your face to the Son." The minister added, "That's exactly what Hylah did."

Marian, a thirteen year old girl, stood at the pulpit during the memorial service to share her heartfelt sympathy for her friend and mentor. Neatly dressed, her shiny black hair was well-coifed and pulled back to show the radiance of her youthful face. She spoke with passion about the lady who had mentored her in the completion of her confirmation class. The congregation, numbering several hundred, was totally amazed at her poise and confidence.

During the reception that followed, I shared my feelings with a group of friends about how I would miss the daily words that Hylah had sent me each morning via e-mail. Within a few weeks an e-mail showed up in my in-box. The subject line said, "Word of the Day." At first, I did not recognize the name and almost deleted the message. But, curiosity got the best of me, so I opened it. There was a page from Webster's Online Dictionary with the Word of the Day.

Unbeknownst to me, Marian had overheard my comments and took some action. Although the messages Hylah had sent were quotes, Bible promises, and words of inspiration, I could not have been more inspired than I was by this young teen's act of compassion.

Later I learned that Marian had received four National Junior Honor Society Awards for community service. She completed one hundred and fifty service hours for the school year. In addition, her Girl Scout troop finished a major part of their Silver Award project in her city. My newest best friend, Marian, is definitely a bright, bold, and beautiful sunflower!

Every detail of the memorial service, right down to the packages of sunflowers seeds each person received, was planned by Hylah. She truly believed in *The Sunflower Principle*. She lived its principles every day of her life. And her legacy lives on in the seeds she sowed.

Lesson 15
What will your legacy be?

CHAPTER 16

THE MYSTERIES AND MIRACLES OF FLOWERS

Many years ago when Mom and Harold (my stepfather who raised me) were young adults, Harold stopped on the side of the road to pick a bouquet of primroses that grow wild in Arkansas. With a silly grin, and expression of his love, he presented the bouquet to Mom. Over the following fifty-something years he would often stop in the spring and pick another bouquet for her. It was a beautiful reminder of his young love. Each time they would laugh and tease each other about that first bouquet. Sadly, he passed away three years ago. It was a very difficult transition for Mom.

One Saturday morning I went out to water the plants and trees, and there in the circle underneath the Crepe Myrtle, next to the patio, was a single primrose standing tall and blooming beautifully. It was not there the day before when I watered the other plants. Of all the places it could have come up in our yard, it was growing next to the little concrete donkey and flower-cart that had belonged to Harold. There it surprisingly grew among an old red antique water pump, a bucket, some unusual rocks, big chunks of Quartz crystal, and a broken flower pot which were all special keepsakes of his.

I ran to get my camera and called to my mom to come out to see the lovely miracle flower. Mother smiled from ear to ear, I could see her eyes glisten. We do believe it was a gift of love from Heaven above.

My dear sunflower friend Hylah had just passed away around Easter time. She was the sunflower to so many in her life. I told Mom, "If we see a single sunflower come up in the yard, I will know it is from Hylah. We both chuckled at the thought and then went on about our day.

Three weeks later, as I was out watering, there by the back gate was a single sunflower about three feet tall. I could not believe my eyes! Of all places for it to show up in the yard, it was right beside a white angel sculpture. I took pictures of course. It had not bloomed yet, but I anxiously waited, watered, inspected, and said many prayers of thanksgiving for this miraculous, big, bold and beautiful sunflower. The primrose and the sunflower were mysterious gifts of love from above.

Lesson 16
Miracles still happen if you have eyes to see.

CHAPTER 17

START THE CONVERSATION

D o you feel you are also called to be a gardener of life? This is your official invitation to join the Sunflower Principle. You only need to plant four little seeds wherever you go. Be encouraging. Anyone can be a cheerleader for someone else who might be struggling or afraid to move forward.

The next time someone you know is ill or perhaps has just experienced a loss of some kind, why not stop by your florist to pick up a single sunflower as a gift. Sunflowers always make people smile. It's a great way to begin the conversation about the Sunflower Principle. The sunflower is a reminder of the powerful lesson that the sun always comes back. Remind them that they too will bloom again.

You may want to make it a practice to send greeting cards that display beautiful pictures of sunflowers to help spread the word about this new practice in your life. Just for fun, throw in a package of sunflower seeds as an extra gift they can plant in the spring.

For those who enjoy cooking, you might try the following recipe for sunflower cookies. They are already unique, but you can add your own special touch with just a little extra effort. You might also enjoy chocolate covered sunflower seeds for something different. Yum!

Remember, this practice is limitless. No matter your age, your health, your financial situation, race, or religion, you can be a vital part of a movement for positive change. Thank you for sharing this dream with me. I hope that you become a gardener of life as you sow your seeds and watch them grow and change your little part of the world.

The four seeds of the Sunflower Principle:
Compassion
Love
Peace
Understanding

May the bouquet of friends you receive over-time
be huge, colorful, exotic, and bright because you
chose to live by the Sunflower Principle.

A Garden of Friendships

There's a garden of lovely friendships,
That I hold precious in my heart.
Each one represents a flower,
Blooming beautifully from the start.

There are roses in every color
There are daisies fun and light.
There are orchids that are exotic,
A special sunflower bold and bright!

When this bouquet of flowers gather
We join our hearts as if only one.
Together we all are fabulous,
And together have so much fun.

Today our petals droop a bit,
Sort of like going through a drought.
For our bold and beautiful sunflower,
Has been feeling down and out.

Each stem in the bouquet of friendships
Gets down on weakened bended knees,
To pray for healing for our sunflower
Who is usually swaying with the breeze.

We are thankful for the seeds she sows
Seeds of joy and laughter brighten our day.
It's because of one beautiful sunflower,
That we fold our hands here to pray.

May God hear our prayers for healing.
May Hylah stand bold and face the Son.
May her enthusiasm be contagious.
And live on in each and everyone.

Donna Austin

Remember that the person who plants few seeds will have a small crop, the one who plants many seeds will have a large crop.
(2 Corinthians 9:6, TEV)

Sunflower Seed Cookies

Preheat oven to 350 degrees
1 cup brown sugar
¾ cup sugar
1 cup butter
1 teaspoon pure vanilla extract
2 eggs
2 cups flour
1 teaspoon baking soda
½ teaspoon salt
½ teaspoon baking powder
2 cups old fashioned oats
1 cup shelled sunflower seeds

Mix first five ingredients in a large mixing bowl and blend well on low speed. Mix next four ingredients together then place in mixer with other ingredients. Once blended, slowly add oats and sunflower seeds

Drop by ice cream scoop onto ungreased cookie sheet, press center down with fork. Cookies will be large like sunflowers. Bake 15 to 18 minutes for large cookies, 10 to 12 minutes for smaller ones. Cool on wire rack.

For variations of this recipe, try adding a little yellow food coloring to the large cookies or add miniature chocolate chips or flaked coconut.

For larger cookies use small fruit scoop.

Live Large:
Live by the Sunflower Principle

Contact Author and Purchase Information

Please visit www.sunflowerprinciple.com
donna@sunflowerprinciple.com

Available through major book sellers or the publisher.

Please call 866-697-5313 ext. 5013 for additional information.

Acknowledgments

I am so blessed to have this special time in life to spend with my eighty-five year old mother. Because of her constant support and encouragement, I have had the time and space to finish this project. She has been my life-long example of compassion, generosity and love. Thank you, Mom!

My grandmother, Ma, inspired me as a little girl to love all people everywhere. Because of her teaching, I amhonored to have friends in almost all nationalities. She is long gone now from my daily life, but the lessons she taught and the way she lived continue to inspire me. Our family is a mosaic of many talents, skills, and knowledge. I'm thankful for each and every family member and for their encouragement and inspiration. My children Chris and Robbye bring so much joy to my life as well as encouragement in my writing. My children and my best friend Michael have been my constant cheerleaders.

When Sri first sent me the e-mail message saying, "You are just like a sunflower in the lives of others," she had no idea what would evolve from that lovely compliment. It is because of Sri that I have found and recognized many other sunflowers among my friends and even found them in perfect strangers. The Good Eggs, The WOW's, The Sunday School Ladies, and Writers' Ink, our creative writing group, have all been a source of inspiration and constant encouragement. They all truly live by the Sunflower Principle. Pat and Ron Looney are among those whom I call dear friends. I appreciate the time they spent reading my manuscript and helping me get it to the point of submitting it to the publisher then encouraging me to follow through to make my dream come true.

Biblography

Books:
  Eiseley, Loren. The Star Thrower 1979 A Harvest/HBJ Book
  The Holy Bible – New King James Version – Thomas Nelson
  Good News Bible – Today's English Version - American Bible
    Society 1966

Songs:
  The Peace Song by Sy Miller and Jill Jackson
  Jesus Loves the Little Children by C. Herbert Woolston

Websites:
  www.brainyquote.com
  www.ewtn.com
  www.madd.org
  www.mckinseyquarterly.com
  www.merriam-webster.com